Turn

Uttered Chaos

First U.S. edition 2013

Editor and Publisher: Laura LeHew

Proofreaders: Quinton Hallett
Josva Halseide
Nancy Carol Moody
Bonnita Stahlberg

Cover art for

© Can Stock Photo Inc. / yurumi

www.utteredchaos.org

Copyright © 2013 Uttered Chaos

All Rights Reserved. Except for brief passages quoted in a newspaper, magazine, radio or television review, no portion of this book may be reproduced in any form or by any means, electronic or mechanical, including photocopying and recording, or by any information storage and retrieval system, without written permission from the Publisher. All rights to the works printed herein remain with the author.

ISBN-13: 978-0-9889366-0-7

CONTENTS

Cheryl Loetscher, SPARE PARTS 1
Quinton Hallett, HER WRISTS 2
Sharon Lask Munson, WINTER REFLECTIONS 3
Tim Pfau, HOTEL BELOVED 4
Marisa Petersen, SOARE CU DINTI 6
Amy Miller, AFTER HEAVY SNOW, FEBRUARY 7
Liz Nakazawa, FATE OF RAIN 8
Laura LeHew, I LOVE YOU MAYBE MORE 9
Shawn T. Boyle, ALMOST EQUINOX 10
Kathleen Cain, LETTERS FROM THE FIELD 11
Quinton Hallett, WAXING YEAR 12
Kathryn Ridall, SPRING IN OREGON
   IS LIKE A BAD BOYFRIEND 13
Charles F. Thielman, WAKING IN APRIL 14
Rick McMonagle, APRIL, AGAIN 15
Tim Pfau, PRAYER FOR A HOLY DAY OF OBLIGATION 16
Cheryl Loetscher, GHOSTS, HAVING NO MAPS 17
Laura Gamache, ODD ISN'T IT 18
Eileen Dawson Peterson, MEMORIAL DAY 19
Bonnita Stahlberg, MOUNT JUNE IN MAY 20
Catherine McGuire, JUNE MORNING, GREENING 22
Marilyn Johnston, JULY FOURTH 24
Quinton Hallett, DÉFENSE DE FUMER 25
Amy Miller, BOYFRIEND WEATHER 26
Ellaraine Lockie, RIPE AT HARVEST 27

Susan Kenyon, LIVING WITH HISTORY 28
Sharon Lask Munson, OFF CENTER OF SAFE......................29
Nancy Carol Moody, MEMPHIS: AUGUST, 1968 31
Amy MacLennan, TURN..32
Caitlin Walsh, WAITING IN THE DARK 33
Laura Gamache, ALL HALLOW'S EVE......................................35
Jose Angel Araguz, OCTOBER 36
Nancy Carol Moody, I'M NOT LIKE YOU THINK I AM...........37
Amy MacLennan, NOVEMBER, LATE.......................................38
J.I. Kleinberg, NOVEMBER 39
Lydia Foster, OVERLAY 41
Kit Sibert, SUGAR 42
Marie Buckley, MID-DECEMBER 43
Ayelet Amittay, LANDSCAPE WITH ANIMATED DEER 45
Jose Angel Araguz, SNOW IN DECEMBER.............................46

ACKNOWLEDGMENTS 48
CONTRIBUTORS 49
INDEX 54

INTRODUCTION

Welcome to a new anthology from Uttered Chaos.

The theme is "months of the year." I left it to the poets to decipher what that meant and was not disappointed. In *Living with History* Susan Kenyon shows us a 1936 Nagasaki. Amy MacLennan's *Turn* ("it blows surrender. It blows forget") beautifully illustrates what happens when things change, and Sharon Lask Munson brings us both the anniversaries of tragedies and sublime white winter camellias.

From Día de los Muertos to Mount June, the drop of the Waterford ball at midnight to conversations with the wind, a poem written to a new bride to a 13-year-old girl waiting to be kissed—lyrical or narrative, the poets write the landscape of the months.

These poems whisper and shout. Read them silently and then go back and read them out loud. Poetry flourishes.

Laura

Cheryl Loetscher

SPARE PARTS

March and April the face is a two-legged camera with bellows, all planes and pouches: hypothetical seat of magical thinking.

May the eyes are mirrors from before the Cambrian explosion. Lash by lash they cup and spill caustic water.

June the feet are sleepwalkers, drowsy pigeons inspecting the world from unfamiliar roosts.

By July the feet sidle away from the flock, unable to grip in narrow places. Senselessly printing the asphalt.

August and September the tongue is a motionless ocean. A secret door. Tedious and unworthy.

October the hands are bluefish and pelicans, picked over by sand crabs, their numbers diminishing.

By November the hands are orphans, accomplices of the bread baker. Thread spinners, flightless as silkworms.

December and January the heart is a row of moored punts, a basket of Amalfi lemons, a stack of beetroot.

February the body, viewed through a rip in the canvas, rises up lithe and rangy from the mauve settee, casts long shadows out beyond the old growth.

Quinton Hallett

HER WRISTS

are glass, Pyrex, tempered
by tapping on church doors.
Her mission: Brinks trucks toting
immutable sparks of treasure fresh off the pyre.
She tucks unmet needs
into glassine envelopes,
lets one seed at a time spill
from a torn corner.
She bloats the flash of circumstance
to bleed blink pop breed.
A Manhattan, all fists,
she could be the New Year's baby, fired up,
refracting too much noise and light
when the Waterford ball drops.

Sharon Lask Munson

WINTER REFLECTIONS

We select a table for two
by the window—a stone's toss
from the café's crackling open fire.

The clear glass beside us
sends back a dueling image—
the blaze within intermingles with

December's white winter camellias
blooming beyond the pane—dense bouquets
of glassy leaves, fragile petals.

Bowed by relentless rain
on this cold, wet New Year's Eve—
the flame, like a cunning serpent

sheds his skin and consumes.

Tim Pfau

HOTEL BELOVED

Hotel Nthatuoa, Beloved, waits on Africa's spine
for travelers from somewhere else to beyond,
with a January summer river washing the feet of the mountain
who spreads her wings in protective cover over beloved,
    Nthatuoa.

Nthatuoa, beloved daughter gone now from the sight
of corn and cattle. Nthatuoa, their beloved daughter, gone.

Where travelers rest and heal, the travelers you would
expect to find in Qacha's Nek, Lesotho (where you
did not expect to travel, so why would they?);
lovers, foreign workers and village girls with jobs in town.

Nthatuoa, beloved daughters on their own now, lonely and proud,
risen to working with bank's crisp paper, listening to cattle low
    outside.

Red bricked, with one rose bush, Hotel Nthatuoa, Beloved,
named for a daughter who died, death you steeled yourself
to accept before you came here, before you even learned
she lived, even though you knew all sons and daughters die.

But not your own beloved daughter, a volunteer
taller now, asleep in a room beyond, tan limbs tangled.

Hotel Nthatuoa where you lie between sheets or
purge traveler's flu into familiar white porcelain through the night
hearing the endless songs, 500 roosters calling and responding
on erotic dreams while 100 dogs, surely yellow, chant the Bass.

Then comes a quiet time while your own beloved
spouse finally sleeps, breathing healing mountain air,
in Nthatuoa's soft embrace so cool next to your own.
You listen to the silence before Lesotho's summer dawn.

No urban sounds at all disturb the clear far bells and distant
laughter that pull you gently from your bed to go out and wash
yourself in beloved Africa's morning greeting to you
uprooted and foreign man, so old, so self contained and calm.

You look across the river and lift your eyes to the gold line
just cracking the arching edge of mountain and hear
the slow fall of beloved goat's bells and herdsman's call
flow down the mountain's rocks to greet the morning water.

Marisa Petersen

SOARE CU DINTI

Fresh heavy snowfall blankets and muffles
the Carpathian countryside, creates
a desert of white dunes.

The laser-intense sun fuses
the bright ceiling of January
to the mountain background,
the horizon blurs and dissolves
in a sea of light.

The golden flare also chisels
shadows into drifts and ravines, defines
ancient Dacian terraces
on steep cultivated slopes.

   Soare cu dinți. The sun bites.

Minus twelve centigrade freeze-frames
everything in this snowscape, everything except
three sheepdogs who leap and circle round
their stock-still flock clumped together
for warmth.

From a nearby tree a crow scolds
the bouncy guard dogs,
but his caw ices up
in mid-air.

The dogs will hear
the crow's complaint
when the thaw
comes.

Amy Miller

AFTER HEAVY SNOW, FEBRUARY

My bootprints
back and forth across the yard
mingled with
a dog's

        he burst in
        through the pickets'
        back gap
        black lab
        white chest
        head up
        and
        headlong
        stopped
        to poop in a corner, saw me

standing there
holding a saw
over the dead
limb
of birch that smashed
the fence

        he fixed me
                with both eyes
        ran
                back out
                into the pines

Liz Nakazawa

FATE OF RAIN

It's Imbolc, February second, and we're
at the refuge. You point out
differences between ducks: coots and mallards and
when I ask you if you believe in prayer
you don't say a thing.

Like the Gaelics, I silently
welcome a bit more of light's return.
But the Pagans did more
on this cross-quarter day of smithcraft and healing:
If it was foul weather the Cailleach hag
gathered firewood and tried spotting serpents
emerging from winter dens.
If clear, she slept in to declare an early spring.

You pull me back to cattails and nutria.
We spy a golden eagle
land and devour prey:
a flash of red, an open belly
and the bird oblivious to time of year.

Laura LeHew

I LOVE YOU MAYBE MORE

"Though lovers be lost love shall not; and death shall have no dominion." Dylan Thomas

in the month of dripping diamonds
and deep dark chocolates
you sidle up—your hand on my
shoulder—the tender squeeze sliding
too close and
closer
two winter-weight shirts away

in the month of candy hearts
you smell like clover
promise berry and bramble
press ever so softly
against my ribs
the knife just beginning
to drip

Shawn T. Boyle

ALMOST EQUINOX

...And the twilight reveals a dark world—
sky water,
wild grass,
high on hills
        soldiering
                the
                      down
                              winds.
Moving together as a scream.
Late winter in March is naked—
lifeless and brown—
then;
In shock from the first gulps of air.
The first to crawl out of the sea.
The first to open its eyes.
The first to really see.

Kathleen Cain

LETTERS FROM THE FIELD

Walking downfield.
Was it March? Beneath

a stilt-work of yucca,
bones relaxed in a semi-circle.

Almost sweet, this little death
of jackrabbit.

Out in the open.
Far from the nearest burrow.

No sign of struggle or chase.
No hawk's methodical ripping

of seams. No skin or fur.
Only an alphabet of bones

curved in slight relief: C
of the spine, elliptical O

of skull and jaw
still attached. The I's

of leg and tail. Message
poised in ease, crouched

in cactus windbreak; every
intention to wait out the storm.

Quinton Hallett

WAXING YEAR

Magnolia buds fatten, camellias, too
in January's false spring.

An older daughter who doesn't know
better, misses two periods

and we hover or hide, unsure
how to suppress the inconvenient news.

A grandchild's already in flower,
her red river poised at the tender gate.

When an ice storm strikes
in February, we rush with blankets

to cover innocent shrubs before they clench
and calla lily spikes before they glaze.

By March, the women are secure,
blood flowing for one, not yet for the other,

and the calla slips easily out of its icy cloak,
the magnolia opens its pursed lips.

Kathryn Ridall

SPRING IN OREGON IS LIKE A BAD BOYFRIEND

he arrives with a handful of daffodils
beams a come hither smile
blazing with heat and promise

you throw off your clothes
sink into his arms

but soon his eyes ice over
his lips curl with disdain

oh yes, he plants a kiss or two
on your winter lips but never
brings the steady love you need

too often he disappears
over the horizon, embraces
some undeserving tart

while you hunker down
with your cat and your flannel sheets

you pray for strength
to remain remote and unimpressed
the next time he comes to town

you know the truth—you will fall
for him again and again

Charles F. Thielman

WAKING IN APRIL

Wave-crests
    like the faces
    of sleeping poets

        bisect my soul.

Dream's warm shirt
                unbuttoned

        and coaxed off my shoulders
        below pre-dawn birdsongs,

        her scent rivers inside
           my tongue

        and floods my chest.

Rick McMonagle

APRIL, AGAIN

Snow level drops
valley streams rush
feverish magnolias
constantly blush
and I cringe, again,
at how badly I treat myself
over the tiniest of tragedies.
And, what about you?
Do I hold you any better
or do I assume the obvious,
and throw up
my hands,
walk away,
read the paper,
plant radishes?
It is now,
After all, April,
Again, a triple "A" rating
and I bet,
if Roberto Clemente
were Alive
he'd be hitting
Another grapefruit
league triple
squeezing out-of-shape
opponents.
April does that to people,
throws a kink in their monotony,
launches another dillydally
in their daily deliberations
when they should be working,
creating a knack,
falling over themselves
for someone.

Tim Pfau

PRAYER FOR A HOLY DAY OF OBLIGATION

Saint Hugh of Grenoble (1053 to eternity),
intercede for this sinner and protect me from my daughter,
on the dark eve of this your sacred, holy feast day, April first.
If it pleases God, shield me from that child's idea of "jokes."

Let all traps be foiled, not sprung. Let my clocks be untouched in
    black
night's timeless sleep. May tight wound spring-loaded buzzer boxes
    marked
"Rattlesnake eggs" be unopened and heavy cans marked "mixed
    nuts"
never be for they never are. Let no openings be sewn,
not cuffs, nor sox, sleeves, bed sheets or purses. Keep my coffee
    safe.

Bless us with cold and hot water lines still in appointed place
and keep rubber bands from the spray hose's handle in the sink.
Let water stay in toilets and keep Vaseline from their seats,
which I beseech you to protect from unbolting in the night.

Anoint sugar and salt with correct labeling. Leave Jell-O
powder in boxes unmoved to shower heads or shaving cups.
Let no surprises be, alive or not, in my daily bread
and save my tobacco products from all her planned explosions.

Such judgments are His alone, so ask God to let banana
pudding in her shoes be unmoved to mine come the morning's
    light.

Amen.

Cheryl Loetscher

GHOSTS, HAVING NO MAPS

Come late at night in pollen-
dusted coveralls while we're sleeping,

slap one another in jest and park
right in front of the steamer trunks,

moaning in harmony like soffit
vents in April squalls, then drift away.

Though we never actually see them,
our impression is they could eat a man whole,

hunkered around bonfires flaming in the fields,
feasting on ribs and fibulae. They find it hard to relax

in two different worlds, some graver task ahead.

Laura Gamache

ODD ISN'T IT

to have emerged from that dark Eden
to rise and ebb no matter how
we cordon off and bargain.

It's summer with the heat high, gray sky,
trees shaking leaves at every passing car.
How far we have driven past our welcome.

We say never again, and then repeat. Coyote
lolls in arbor's shade, and we are filled
with anxiety, and sad seedless watermelon.

Eileen Dawson Peterson

MEMORIAL DAY

Little flags wave here and there
across the rolling lawns
bouquets of spring's first flowers
in memory of ones who've gone.

The sun breaks through the clouds
sparkles dew drops on the grass.
People passing to and fro
wait for their pain to pass.

Every year it is the same
as every year before
remembering friends and family
missing them once more.

It is a task we cherish
a love act so dear
remembering the loved ones
remembering every year.

Bonnita Stahlberg

MOUNT JUNE IN MAY

Savor the Oregon wild,
arrive early
at the base of Mount June;
delight in the first spring view:

sword ferns with shiny leather blades
nudge white trillium fly-wheels
and yellow-green oxalis leaves,
shamrocks, tart to taste.

My hiker's heart races.

The crest trail climbs,
switchbacks to the ridge.
Sluggish from dormant winter,
I wonder about bears:

how fast do they move
hours after hibernation?
will they pause to munch
the pink currants untouched by deer?

The rhodies aren't quite ready
(and neither am I),
no worry to the caterpillar
savoring minutes, seconds,

crossing my boot on summit shale
above a forest of Douglas fir.
A marker from the '30s lookout site
recalls sky dwellers who inhaled fog,

waited for those first clearings:
the Willamette River Valley—
Mount Hood to Diamond Peak;
Bachelor Butte, the Sisters in the east.

Catherine McGuire

JUNE MORNING, GREENING
—after Wallace Stevens

I

As morning breathes its musk of basil,
fir, morel, lilac, sage
and birdsong migrates, tree to tree

and greens mutate past counting:
deep jade, celadon, celery, moss—
how not to lose the thread of tasks

winter-hoarded, primed to surge
the summer toward productive climax?
Not just pollen dulls the will

and sets intent a-tipsy; not just sun
bleaches thoughts to bone-white pause,
to limpid bud that soaks up dawn.

II

As morning spritzes perfume: thyme,
rosemary, clover, new-turned earth—
and birdsong's improv fills the trees

and greens compete in four divisions:
freshness, clarity, uniqueness, verve—
how not to fall behind in tasks

delineated, urgent, framing
summer as industrious oeuvre?
Not just riverhum lulls the muscles

and jellies the resolve; not just flicker's
staccato hammers weight to rising plans
and sinks limbs in morning's skiff.

III

As morning swirls its languorous potion
of cut grass, compost, apple
and birds' arpeggios fledge their nests

and greens transmute sun to lifeblood
drinking light in emerald hunger
how not to lust for such a mouth, such tasks—

a verdant alchemy: to pollinate
the juicy summer to a ripened fruit?
Not just breeze sets heart to flutter

and tug at ties; not just olive shadow
cuts logic into leafy shreds and
glazes dream on stoneware obligation.

IV

As morning plays its ghost blue theme
of lavender and young roses
and birdsong punctuates the cedar's phrase

and greens rewrite the land's long
winter elegy to lyrical delight
how not to count the outlined tasks

as trite, superfluous, jamming
summer into ill-fitting lines?
Not just leaf fall slides the moment

into freeform; not just pearl hilled cloud
nudges ambition cockeyed, wins
my consent to be revised.

Marilyn Johnston

JULY FOURTH

He can't let go of the image:
rocket and artillery rounds lighting up the sky
overhead, blasts reflecting off Thu Bon River;
the incessant rattling of earth, and at dawn,
the hunks of shrapnel that shredded his tent walls,
missing his body by inches.

He figured he'd survived this long,
and, Hell, wouldn't it be downright cruel
to take him now, after nineteen months
in 'Nam and just hours before
his discharge, a plane taking him
far away from Da Nang.

He says it didn't take long to become
a fatalist—to believe the only thing separating
those who lived and those who died was luck—
particularly during days on jungle patrol
in 120-degree heat.
Sweat rolling down like hate.

But God knows, he still can't shake it.

Each summer for the past thirty-two years,
he tells me that story as we sit on the grassy
Willamette River bank—then silently wait
for the first boom, the first blast,
the lights brightening up
the night sky.

Quinton Hallett

DÉFENSE DE FUMER

They didn't see the sign
No sparks were left either
No sizzling down
No ember jamais
They could see nothing
explicit posted on the balconies
of all those high rise grattes-ciels

Their honeymoon year
the move to Paris
they both chain smoked
She'd straddle chairs backwards
& he would lean seductively
against door jambs tapping ash into his palm

They swore they could hear comets falling

On Bastille Day twelve summers later
she leaned over packing boxes
an unlit Gauloise hanging from her lips

She underscored her maiden name with a marker
separated out her share of the feux d'artifices

The air conditioner ticked off
hours till sundown

Amy Miller

BOYFRIEND WEATHER

For Gina, it's July,
bookstalls baking
on sun-white sidewalks
off Geary, a good man
tall off her bare
left shoulder, her leather bag
stocked for the season:
sunglasses, toothbrush,
tear gas, a jacket
just in case.

Ellaraine Lockie

RIPE AT HARVEST

She's 13 and pure as the Montana air she breathes
He's a bronze and muscled 16
A kid on the road with his Oklahoma uncles
Come in August to harvest her family's wheat
Asks *Any of y'all wash and iron shirts*
She'll make her mother stay up an extra
two hours to learn

She keeps the pile in her room overnight
Has trouble sleeping and when she does
Dreams of riding on the slow rock
of a black stallion's back
She won't know the word *pheromone*
until she follows her first boyfriend to college

Here and now she knows only that she wants
to deliver all their lunches to the combine crew
They take her to the county fair on Sunday
When even wheat bursting from its beards
has to learn to wait
That night on the Ferris wheel
the Oklahoma Kid takes her hand in his
Starts one of those brushfires that gets
out of control real fast in August

She's ready for this, been practicing
on her pillow since she was 10
and saw Rock Hudson kiss Doris Day
But then Oklahoma asks if he can collect
his shirts in the morning
before they move on to the next farm
Steam rising at midnight

Susan Kenyon

LIVING WITH HISTORY

You tell me
this is the greatest country.
The flame of shame rises in me

as it did in 1936
at the inn where we stayed
in Nagasaki:

the first Japanese city
to host Europeans
three hundred years earlier.

There I was told
by my little sister
that she and her gang

had stashed the greatest pile
of pinecones to attack
our host's children.

We apologized. Later

another American passing by
shot their pet king snake
as we children watched it

drinking milk.
Nine years later
we dropped the greatest bomb.

Sharon Lask Munson

OFF CENTER OF SAFE

I

Tragedies have anniversaries—
ten years later we remember September 11th
two planes crashing into the World Trade Center
police and firemen rushing into the blaze
ordinary citizens running
       fabric over their mouths
              coated in dust, debris.

II

Soon we will walk through
newly revamped airports
shoes in one hand, identification in the other
queues of travelers, heading
to the Advanced Imaging Technology Scanner Chambers—
       assured we can be confident
             only our generic outlines will be revealed.

III

We will all die. When or how is the question.
Viewing the world through fear
      shapes our lives
           drives us mad.

IV

Central Missouri, corn, wheat, soybeans
pie auctions, tractor shows
4th of July celebrations.
Autumn leaves, angle of moonlight
    parents tuck in children,
        listen to prayers.

A short distance away
Whitman Air Force Base
and the 509th Bomb Wing
    Global Strike Command,
        home of the Stealth Bombers.

Nancy Carol Moody

MEMPHIS: AUGUST, 1968

Probably it was the heat that drove us out of the house to sprawl across the picnic table where water dripped from lemonade glasses beading the red-checked oilcloth.

Later we flapped that cloth like a white sheet, the water shattering over our squealing half-nakedness to scatter in directions we could not see because we were forbidden to look at the sun.

We believed in threatened blindness. The camera's flashed bulbs, blown and melted in their blue hot cubes, had shown us what it meant to see too much light.

At dusk we could not help but stare at the shrub's growing luminance. And then the rhinestones unpinned themselves to become the fireflies we crushed in our palms.

Amy MacLennan

TURN

The air is turning today. Even
with scorching weeks,
a month of summer ahead,
a skeletal-tree wind slings
early winter on an August afternoon.
Across browned grasses
it blows surrender. It blows forget.
I button my coat,
wipe dust from my stinging eyes,
a season thrown full across my reluctant back.

Caitlin Walsh

WAITING IN THE DARK

On hot, close nights
we sit on the roofs of cars, under the golden cat's-eye
    moon,
lie on our backs and watch for stars escaping,
coming loose from the net
and plummeting to earth.
We trace their winding filaments with our fingertips,
whispering their beautiful names to the darkness:
Cygnus, Orion, Draco, Gemini.

We sit on winding streets in the late September heat,
winding streets beyond the outskirts of town
where there are no houses,
only flat lands full of dusty weeds,
turning mellow gold as summer begins to die,
shining in the reflected glow
of headlights.

Others pass us, driving too fast,
on the long road to their own
dark and deserted roads, on the edges of the city.
Our paired shadows
grow huge and dark in their headlights,
then slowly collapse,
fade to nothingness again.

We sit on the roofs of cars,
making plans we will not follow,
making promises
that fade away with the shadows
when the dawn comes.

We watch for stars to fall,
one moment of light and heat and beauty,
followed by a long time spent
cold and waiting in the dark.

Laura Gamache

ALL HALLOW'S EVE

Sweets tribes ring our bell, wear ills
they do not feel—a bloody wound
half-peeled, black goo for absent tooth.

Life entails too few performances.
Shout and carry on! Too soon we're gone.
Glug your flagons. Pry messy seeds

from Cinderellas. Our children
walk forward with lanterns, heads
whirled like sugar around a paper cone.

O Crones! Kiss us with wax lips
and dollop our throats with sugar blood.
Candy kiss in a paper bag, a pumpkin's

sunken smile. Mold is black art too,
and potions not all that set in motion
spells that crackle upwards in the night.

Jose Angel Araguz

OCTOBER

No one claims responsibility
for the shriveled flowers

the willow drops leaves
whose bodies will never be found

the wind comes through
holding conversation with itself

you can almost hear
dust stir

writing out a notice
and placing it all over the forest

Nancy Carol Moody

I'M NOT LIKE YOU THINK I AM

This late November light—
liquid minerals sluicing / through panes
puddles gridded impossibly / to walls

This close / to evening
angles and physics preventing
the presumptive pools / on floor

Even the cat understands
the need / to move on—
he soaked up his piece earlier / in the day
when it still contained
a useful warmth

Out / in the field
/ beyond the window—
a woman, wandering the weeds
/ in her dark long coat

The dog she keeps / for company
leaps in arcs / above tops / of fading grass
The woman looks / to her feet
walks her tighter
and tighter circles

—If you believe the passing light
says something / about the way
a day can turn itself inside out

—if you think a woman walking
by herself / in a field
is loneliness

you are wrong

Amy MacLennan

NOVEMBER, LATE

The rains arrive. They'll stick
until next May. Time now
for cold bathroom floors, damp entryways,
the dry hack. Ends of day sliced down,
the trees just seem to shake.
And I wait.
              Before she died,
I gave her flowers (a wash of roses)
or sweets. Candies, toffee, fudge.
Things of the moment. Nothing
that lasted. Her language fading away,
she called when she got a bouquet.
Two yellows, one white, three reds,
a pink, a yellow, a red...
Lost count. Forgot.
Started over.
              And the wet leaves
stick to my porch, my steps.
Slick, they soak a shape shadow
to the cement. Each day shifts the pattern.
And the rain washes.
              Her favorite
were the raspberry creams. Dark chocolate
and smooth pink center. She'd bite,
chew slowly, finish one off. Carefully
crumple the wrapper. Look into the box
for another.
              Daylight will come back
with new leaf folds on the tips
of branches. I watch for them
even now, even as the dying ones remain.

J.I. Kleinberg

NOVEMBER

the way it starts with No
then sends its charcoal shroud
its Scorpio storms
to tear at us with icy teeth
to scour roots and hurl trees
rip fences from their posts

my father fades

it starts with No
the night's long dark
the lowered sky
and cardboard trees
the crusted roads
a motorcade

my father fades

it starts with No
then drenches fallowed fields
with slaughter's carcass
soldiers' blood
limbs snapped before
the starving wind

my father fades

it starts with No
my father fades
my father's grave

an autumn husk
a smothered flame—
the way it ends

in ember.

Lydia Foster

OVERLAY

Magenta
rivers of rich color,
more lies.

I cover over the day with paint thick as lava,
too pink to be real. It will say
alive.

Small streams of black drip down the canvas,
make iridescent tributaries,
the colors of a crow's wings.

November sun glancing
through
the picture window.

Kit Sibert

SUGAR

It's the magic, the Aztecan/Catholic
sugar humor, those festive deaths
on Día de los Muertos.

For me, the cookies, the Big Chew, the peanut
butter and jelly sandwich as I lounge on that
cemetery plot overlooking the Umpqua Valley.

Year after year, gazing down at the llamas,
and the cows and the horses.
I'm eating bites of Chips Ahoy and

the little angels, fluttering around like
butterflies and the tiny skulls,
rolling all about.

Marie Buckley

MID-DECEMBER

this is the longest term
one dozen weeks to trip up in
students too young for their children
too broke from so many tattoos
for having nails done every week
iPhones lit in every palm
driving without licenses
bullet casings on campus corners

at the sink in the supply room
we adjuncts wash out yesterday's soup bowls
to heat up today's soup
eyes bloodshot and heads aching
I ask another instructor
if she is working extra hours
it's all extra

I see my students Dante and Amber
practicing descriptive writing
using photographs of each other
their faces mirrors of joy
every word bursting their love
Amber shows me her lunch baggie
fat with radishes red as Santa's suit
mandarin oranges plump as small pumpkins
we've been together for four years

and I suddenly remember
the future unrolling
like a long string of lights
wrapping the most breathtaking tree
every bulb blinking and bright
tinsel embracing evergreen branches

lacy flakes of snow drifting by the window
you and I home with each other
our words sweet and true
as the angel in the sky
above the stable

Ayelet Amittay

LANDSCAPE WITH ANIMATED DEER

Now winter, thorny boughs, the cold
to stand against, everything
visible as breath, near-breaking.
And this herd, their bodies spooled
wire and lights. The rigid bow,
lift, bow of their heads just hammers home
how useless grazing is to them
in their empty frames. Even so,
their faces seem familiar and kind,
and I see myself in the tight
wire armature, studded with lights
that blink and flicker into wind.
They shed their pale glow over the lawn,
casting themselves against the house
and shrubs with a selfless animal grace,
as when, in a predawn blur years gone,
I walked the spine of a hill in the thaw
of another winter's death, and saw
a deer step to the edge of the wood.
I was lit by that flare, the electric blood.

Jose Angel Araguz

SNOW IN DECEMBER

As one fell
and then

another
against

the pane
before him,

he began
to see

in the flakes
the drawn

lines of
eyelashes,

the world now
closing

and closing
its eyes.

ACKNOWLEDGMENTS

Thanks to the editors of the following journals and books in which these poems first appeared:

Amy Miller, "After Heavy Snow, February," *The Mechanics of the Rescue*.
Marilyn Johnston, "July Fourth," *Red Dust Rising*.
Laura LeHew, "I Love You Maybe More," *It's Always Night, It Always Rains*.
Ellaraine Lockie, "Ripe at Harvest," *Ibbetson Street*.
Tim Pfau, "Hotel Beloved," *Gold Man Review*.
Charles F. Thielman, "Waking in April," *What the River Brings*.

CONTRIBUTORS

Ayelet Amittay has an MFA from the University of Michigan—Ann Arbor. She is a nurse practitioner. Her writing will appear in the Orange Lining project: www.orangelining.net.

Jose Angel Araguz hails from Corpus Christi, Texas. His work has appeared in *Hanging Loose* and *Crab Creek Review*, and has been featured in Ted Kooser's *American Life in Poetry*. His chapbook, *The Wall*, was recently published by Tiger's Eye Press. He presently resides in Eugene, Oregon.

Shawn T. Boyle is a sinner, giver, drinker, stinker, worker, husband, son, father, asshole, hard, funny looking, long hair, skinny, color blind poet from Pacific Grove, California. A child of the Midwest, he felt lucky to have the chance to live in wide open spaces. He has attended poetry workshops under Robert Bly. He just got a poem published in *Fault Lines Poetry*.

Marie Buckley works as an adjunct developmental writing instructor at Portland Community College. She is co-author of *Quartet: four poetic voices, Media Weavers 2006*, and leads occasional prose and poetry writing workshops in and around Washington County, Oregon. Marie lives with six parrots, five cats, one husband and as much humor as possible.

Kathleen Cain's poetry has appeared recently in The *Eleventh Muse, Collecting Life: Poets on Objects Known and Imagined*, and *Earth's Daughters #79* (Stormy Weather). She has work forthcoming in *Untidy Seasons: an Anthology of Nebraska Women Poets*. She participated in Interwoven Illuminations, a collaboration between poets and artists at the RANE Gallery in Taos, New Mexico, in 2008 and helped organize a similar event, Look Both Ways, in Lincoln, Nebraska in 2009. She contributes to *The Bloomsbury Review* and is the author of a nonfiction book, *The Cottonwood Tree: An American Champion* (Big Earth Publishing, Boulder, 2007). A native Nebraskan, she lives in Arvada, Colorado.

Lydia Foster graduated from Wichita State University with a double major in psychology and creative writing. She went on to study in the MFA program. She has raised two daughters, helped establish a small business, created ink drawings, and deposited many poems in the mouth of a large black trunk.

Seattle poet and educator **Laura Gamache** has poems recently published or forthcoming in *Clackamas Literary Review*, *South Dakota Review*, and the Winter 2012 issue of the online journal, *Menacing Hedge*. Her chapbook, *nothing to hold onto*, was published by Finishing Line Press in 2005. She was selected as a Jack Straw Foundation writer in 1999 and 2002.

Quinton Hallett writes and edits from Noti, Oregon. She has three chapbooks, is past chair of the Eugene-Springfield Chapter of the Oregon Poetry Association, and her work has appeared or is forthcoming in *The Medulla Review*, *Tiger's Eye*, *Original Weather*, *Collecting Life: Poets on Objects Known and Imagined*, and *Fault Lines*.

Marilyn Johnston is an Oregon writer and filmmaker. Her work has been included in *Calyx*, *Poetry International*, and *Walking Portland's Bridges Using Poetry as a Compass*, among others. She received a Robert Penn Warren writing competition prize, as well as fellowships from Oregon Literary Arts, Fishtrap, and the Barbara Deming Memorial Fund for Women. *Red Dust Rising*, her chapbook of poems about a family healing from War, was nominated for a Pushcart Prize.

Susan Kenyon was born in Shanghai to journalists: a British father and an American mother. She is a poet and a painter but never at the same time. Dressed in American clothes with an American accent, she received her education in British schools and sees herself as not quite part of the group. This duality has influenced her work. Living in her second life, Susan will shortly be in her 90th year.

J.I. Kleinberg works and plays with words. She is co-author of the book *Fat Stupid Ugly: One Woman's Courage to Survive*, is a past winner in the Sue C. Boynton Poetry Contest and blogs most days at chocolateisaverb.wordpress.com. She lives in Bellingham, Washington, and doesn't own a television.

Laura LeHew's poems appear widely in publications such as *Anobium*, *Eleven Eleven*, *FutureCycle: American Society: What Poets See*, *PANK* and *Spillway Magazine*. Collections include: *Beauty* (Tiger's Eye Press); *It's Always Night, It Always Rains* part of the anthology *Ashes Caught on the Edge of Light: 10 Chapbooks* (Winterhawk Press) (09/12) and forthcoming *Willingly Would I Burn* (MoonPath Press). Laura received her MFA from the California

College of the Arts. Laura writes, edits and sharpens her claws in Eugene, Oregon—Uttered Chaos www.utteredchaos.org.

Ellaraine Lockie is a widely published and awarded poet, nonfiction book author and essayist. Her seventh chapbook, *Stroking David's Leg*, was awarded Best Individual Collection for 2010 from *Purple Patch* magazine in England, and her eighth chapbook, *Red for the Funeral*, won the 2010 San Gabriel Poetry Festival Chapbook Contest. Her recent chapbook, *Wild as in Familiar*, from Finishing Line Press received The Aurorean's Chapbook Pick for Spring, 2012. Ellaraine teaches poetry workshops and serves as Poetry Editor for the lifestyles magazine, *Lilipoh*.

Cheryl Loetscher writes from Colorado. Her poems have appeared widely, and a number have won prizes and distinctions in literary contests across the United States. She was awarded the 2008 Douglas Freels Poetry Prize by the FCCJ Writer's Festival, and her first collection of poems, *Unclaimed Baggage*, published by Finishing Line Press in 2007, was awarded the 2008 Jean Pedrick Chapbook Award by the New England Poetry Club.

Amy MacLennan has been published in *Hayden's Ferry Review*, *River Styx*, *Linebreak*, *Cimarron Review*, *Cloudbank*, *Windfall*, *Folio* and *Rattle*. Her chapbook, *The Fragile Day*, was released from Spire Press in the summer of 2011. She also has a chapbook, *Weathering*, that was recently released from Uttered Chaos in Eugene.

Catherine McGuire has had more than 230 poems published in venues such as: *Adagio*, *FutureCycle*, *Green Fuse*, *New Verse News*, *Nibble*, *Portland Lights Anthology* and *Tapjoe*. Her chapbook, *Palimpsests*, was published by Uttered Chaos in 2011. She has two self-published chapbooks. Her website is www.cathymcguire.com.

Rick McMonagle was born and raised in Pittsburgh, PA. He studied with Allen Ginsberg and Anne Waldman at Naropa University where he received a Poetics Certificate. His new chapbook, *Spencer Butte Meditations*, was published by Mountains and Rivers Press. He lives in Portland, Oregon.

Amy Miller's poems have appeared in *Northwest Review*, *Crab Orchard Review*, *Many Mountains Moving*, *Permafrost*, and *ZYZZYVA*. She was chosen by Tony Hoagland as the winner of the Cultural Center of Cape Cod National Poetry Competition and was a finalist for Nimrod's Pablo Neruda Prize and the Bellingham Review 49th Parallel Award. She works as the publications manager for the Oregon Shakespeare Festival.

Nancy Carol Moody's work has appeared or is forthcoming in *Salamander, The MacGuffin, The New York Quarterly, The Carolina Quarterly,* and *The Los Angeles Review.* She is the author of *Photograph With Girls* (Traprock) and has just completed a new manuscript titled *Negative Space*. Nancy lives in Eugene, Oregon, and can be found online at www.nancycarolmoody.com.

Sharon Lask Munson is the author of the chapbook, *Stillness Settles Down the Lane* (Uttered Chaos, 2010) and a full-length book of poems, *That Certain Blue* (Blue Light Press, 2011). She publishes widely in literary journals and anthologies. She grew up in Detroit, Michigan, taught overseas five years with the Department of Defense schools, and taught the next twenty years in Anchorage, Alaska. She is now retired and lives in Eugene, Oregon.

Liz Nakazawa is the editor of *Deer Drink the Moon: Poems of Oregon* (Ooligan Press, 2007), chosen as a "Best Pick" by Powell's and as one of the Best 150 Books of Oregon of the last 150 years, a designation of the Oregon State Library. Her second anthology, *A Knotted Bond: Poets Speak of their Sisters*, will be published by Uttered Chaos. She has freelance written over 300 articles including ones for *The Oregonian, Psychology Today, Christian Science Monitor, Oregon Business Magazine* and *American Health and Fitness.* Her love is teaching book marketing classes to new authors.

For six months of the year **Marisa Petersen** and her husband stick close to home and tend their organic gardens. After making the last batch of blackberry jam and gifting the last zucchinis, they grab their passports and head out to explore other latitudes and longitudes.

Eileen Dawson Peterson lives in Eugene, OR. She has written poetry since childhood. She has been published in several anthologies and publications such as *South Dakota Magazine, The Lutheran Message, Arabesques, Denali, Tiger's Eye,* and *Avocet.* She won honorable mentions for two poems and a play in the 2004 Annual *Writers Digest* Writing Competition. The play, "Blue Skies and Butterflies" was produced 2009. She is the author of *Kitty With the Raccoon Tail* (Dragonfly's Eye Press).

Tim Pfau writes poetry and other things, themed mostly in darkness and light, in Salem, Oregon. His work has appeared in print and on-line journals, newspapers, and multi-media shows. He serves on the Board of the Oregon Poetry Association and can be reached at tjpfau@msn.com.

Kathryn Ridall is the author of two poetry chapbooks and editor of two anthologies, most recently *What the River Brings: Oregon River Poems*. She lectures and teaches workshops on the muse and creative process. Her home is in Eugene where she frequently walks along the Willamette and is editor of the Oregon Poetry Association newsletter. Her website is www.kathryn-ridall.com.

Kit Sibert's work is influenced by her childhood in Mexico, Puerto Rico and Cuba (where she lived from 1950 to 1960) and by her years in New York City, Madrid, Boston, San Francisco, Los Angeles and the Pacific Northwest. Presently in Eugene, Oregon, she works part time as a clinical social worker and participates in numerous poetry groups and poetry readings. She has published *How The Light Gets In* (lulu.com), a book of poetry, paintings and prose, and has poems in *Vivace Magazine* and *Askew*.

An Oregon native, **Bonnita Stahlberg** lives in Eugene. She received her M.A. at the University of Oregon. Her poems have appeared in *Cloudbank*, *Tiger's Eye*, *Windfall* and *Ms. Magazine*. Stahlberg has won state and regional awards, as well as an international contest that took her to Ireland. She enjoys walking, going to films and plays, and humoring her pet chinchilla.

Charles F. Thielman was raised in Charleston, SC, and Chicago, educated at red-bricked universities and on city streets. Charles has worked as a youth counselor, truck driver, city bus driver and enthused bookstore clerk. Married on a Kauai beach in 2011, a loving Grandfather for five free spirits, Charles' inspired work as Poet and shareholder in an independent Bookstore's collective continues! Charles' chapbook, *Into the Owl-Dreamed Night*, a must read, available from Uttered Chaos. www.utteredchaos.org.

Caitlin Walsh is a full-time college student in California. Her poetry has recently appeared in *StepAway Magazine*, *Niteblade Magazine*, and the *2012 Rhysling Anthology*. She was also nominated for the Pushcart Prize. When Caitlin is not writing, she devours good books, explores hard-to-access parts of town, and scavenges local secondhand shops, searching for buried treasure.

INDEX

A

Amittay, Ayelet 45, 49
Araguz, Jose Angel 36, 46, 49

B

Boyle, Shawn T. 10, 49
Buckley, Marie 43, 49

C

Cain, Kathleen 11, 49

F

Foster, Lydia 41, 49

G

Gamache, Laura 18, 35, 50

H

Hallett, Quinton 2, 12, 25, 50

J

Johnston, Marilyn 24, 50

K

Kenyon, Susan 28, 50
Kleinberg, J.I. 39, 50

L

LeHew, Laura 9, 50
Lockie, Ellaraine 27, 51
Loetscher, Cheryl 1, 17, 51

M

MacLennan, Amy 32, 38, 51
McGuire, Catherine 22, 51
McMonagle, Rick 15, 51
Miller, Amy 7, 26, 51
Moody, Nancy Carol 31, 37, 52
Munson, Sharon Lask 3, 29, 52

N

Nakazawa, Liz 8, 52

P

Petersen, Marisa 6, 52
Peterson, Eileen Dawson 19, 52
Pfau, Tim 4, 16, 53

R

Ridall, Kathryn 13, 53

S

Sibert, Kit 42, 53
Stahlberg, Bonnita 20, 53

T

Thielman, Charles F. 14, 53

W

Walsh, Caitlin 33, 54

www.ingramcontent.com/pod-product-compliance
Lightning Source LLC
Chambersburg PA
CBHW061514040426
42450CB00008B/1609